Harry Style
Quiz Book

101 Questions To Test Your Knowledge Of This Incredibly Successful Musician

By Colin Carter

Harry Styles Quiz

This book contains one hundred and one informative and entertaining trivia questions with multiple choice answers. With 101 questions, some easy, some more demanding, this entertaining book will really test your knowledge of Harry Styles.

You will be quizzed on a wide range of topics associated with Harry for you to test yourself; with questions on his early days, his songs, his lyrics, his achievements, his awards and much more, guaranteeing you a truly fun, educational experience.

This quiz book will provide entertainment for fans of all ages and will certainly test your knowledge of this world-famous musician. The book is packed with information and is a must-have for all true Harry Styles fans, wherever you live in the world.

Published by Glowworm Press

7 Nuffield Way

Abingdon OX14 1RL

Disclaimer

ACKNOWLEDGEMENTS

My friend's daughter Lila simply adores Harry Styles.

As a writer, I thought I would write a book on Harry for her to test herself and to see how much she really knows about the legend that he is.

She told me that she was not alone, and that Harry had millions of fans and that I should write the book for every one of them, not just her.

So I did!   This book is for all you wonderful Harry Styles fans – wherever you live in the world.

I do hope you enjoy it.

Colin Carter

Here is the first set of questions.

1. When was Harry born?
   A. 1990
   B. 1992
   C. 1994
   D. 1996

2. What is Harry's star sign?
   A. Aquarius
   B. Aries
   C. Leo
   D. Sagittarius

3. Where was Harry born?
   A. Bloxwich
   B. Droitwich
   C. Nantwich
   D. Redditch

4. What is Harry's middle name?
   A. Eden
   B. Edgar
   C. Edmond
   D. Edward

5. What was Harry's first job?
   A. Bailiff
   B. Baker
   C. Bank Clerk
   D. Barista

6. What was the name of Harry's first band?
   A. White Eagles
   B. White Elephant
   C. White Equestrian
   D. White Eskimo

7. Which TV show did Harry gain fame in?
   A. Britain's Got Talent
   B. Pop Idol
   C. The Voice
   D. The X Factor

8. Which judge suggested Harry become part of a boy band rather than going solo?
   A. Simon Cowell
   B. Sharon Osborne
   C. Nicole Scherzinger
   D. Louis Walsh

9. What was the name of the band that they formed?
   A. False Direction

B. Mis Direction
C. One Direction
D. Wrong Direction

10. Which instrument does Harry play?
    A. Drums
    B. Guitar
    C. Piano
    D. All the above

Here are the answers to the first ten questions. If you get seven or more right, you are doing very well so far, but the questions will get harder.

A1. Harry Styles was born on February 1st, 1994.

A2. Harry's star sign Is Aquarius. Specifically, he is noted as an eccentric Aquarius Sun with a charming Libra Moon!

A3. Harry Styles was born in the town of Redditch in Worcestershire, England. He later moved to Holmes Chapel in Cheshire during his childhood.

A4. Edward is Harry's middle name.

A5. Harry's first job was as a baker. He worked part time in a bakery in Holmes Chapel when he was 16 years old.

A6. Harry made his start in music at Holmes Chapel Comprehensive School, where he was the lead singer of a band called White Eskimo.

A7. Harry gained fame via the reality TV show "The X Factor" in 2010. He auditioned for "The

X Factor" as a solo artist but was later grouped with other contestants to form a boy band.

A8. Nicole Scherzinger suggested that Harry along with Liam Payne, Louis Tomlinson, Niall Horan and Zayn Malik form a boy band.

A9. That's an easy one. One Direction was of course the name of the band that was formed.

A10. Harry is known for playing multiple instruments, including drums, guitar and piano.

Here is the next set of questions.

11. What was Harry's solo debut single called?
    A. Kiwi
    B. Lights Up
    C. Sign Of The Times
    D. Two Ghosts

12. What did Harry want to be to when he was young?
    A. An accountant
    B. A doctor
    C. A lawyer
    D. A surveyor

13. What is Harry's favourite TV show?
    A. Friends
    B. Game Of Thrones
    C. Star Trek
    D. The Traitors

14. Which member of One Direction does Harry have a strong friendship with?
    A. Niall Horan
    B. Zayn Malik
    C. Liam Payne
    D. Louis Tomlinson

15. Which magazine featured Harry on its cover wearing a dress?
    A. GQ
    B. Harpers Bazaar
    C. Elle
    D. Vogue

16. Who designed the dress that Harry wore?
    A. JW Anderson
    B. Marc Jacobs
    C. Ralph Lauren
    D. Alexander McQueen

17. What was the title of Harry's debut album?
    A. Harry Here
    B. Harry Styles
    C. I Am Harry
    D. My Name Is Harry

18. When was Harry's debut album released?
    A. 2016
    B. 2017
    C. 2018
    D. 2019

19. How many nipples does Harry have?

A. 1
B. 2
C. 3
D. 4

20.What was Harry's first number one single on the Billboard Hot 100 chart?
   A. Adore You
   B. Golden
   C. Sign Of The Times
   D. Watermelon Sugar

Here are the answers to the last set of questions.

A11. Harry's debut solo single was "Sign of the Times," which was released in April 2017. It is a powerful ballad that showcases his vocal range and song writing abilities.

A12. Harry wanted to be a lawyer when he was a youngster.

A13. Harry's favourite TV show is Friends. He has said that he loves the humour and the characters.

A14. Harry and Louis Tomlinson developed a strong bond during their time in One Direction and have maintained a close friendship ever since.

A15. Harry appeared on the cover of Vogue magazine wearing a dress for the December 2020 issue, provoking conversations about gender norms in fashion. Harry made history by becoming the first solo male cover in Vogue magazine's 127-year history. He wore a dress showcasing his unique style and breaking gender norms in the fashion industry and showcasing his unique style.

A16. JW Anderson designed the dress that Harry wore on the cover of Vogue magazine, making a statement about embracing gender-fluid fashion and breaking traditional gender norms.

A17. Harry's debut solo album was self-titled, simply named "Harry Styles".

A18. Harry's debut album "Harry Styles" was released in 2017, a year after One Direction went on an indefinite hiatus.

A19. Harry has 4 nipples, a condition known as polythelia. While most might think it's quite rare, specialists have revealed that polythelia is actually not that uncommon at all, and a lot of people don't even know they have it.

A20. "Watermelon Sugar" became Harry's first solo number-one hit on the Billboard Hot 100 chart

Here is the next set of questions.

21. What was the title of Harry's debut solo tour?
    A. Late On Tour
    B. Lips On Tour
    C. Live On Tour
    D. Love On Tour

22. What colour eyes does Harry have?
    A. Blue
    B. Brown
    C. Green
    D. Hazel

23. Which song earned Harry his first Grammy award?
    A. Adore You
    B. Falling
    C. Lights Up
    D. Watermelon Sugar

24. What was the title of the autobiographical style book written by Sean Smith in 2021?
    A. The Making Of A Legend
    B. The Making Of A Modern Man
    C. The Making Of A Musician
    D. The Making Of A Unique Talent

25. When did Harry co-host the Met Gala alongside Lady Gaga?
    A. 2017
    B. 2019
    C. 2021
    D. 2023

26. What was the title of Harry's second album?
    A. Dead Line
    B. Fine Line
    C. Life Line
    D. Pipe Line

27. What tattoo has Harry got on his stomach?
    A. Bat
    B. Bear
    C. Bison
    D. Butterfly

28. Where did Harry get his first tattoo?
    A. Arm
    B. Back
    C. Leg
    D. Neck

29. What tattoo has Harry got on his chest?
    A. Skylarks
    B. Sparrows
    C. Starlings
    D. Swallows

30. What roulette number tattoo has Harry got?
    A. Red 7
    B. Red 19
    C. Black 17
    D. Black 31

Here is the latest set of answers.

A21. Harry's debut solo tour was titled "Harry Styles - Live On Tour". The two-part tour began with intimate venues in 2017 and continued to arenas in 2018.

A22. Harry has declared that his eye colour is "green, with a bit of yellow and light brown in there"!

A23. "Watermelon Sugar" won Harry his first Grammy Award in 2021 - for Best Pop Solo Performance.

A24. The title of the autobiographical style book written by Sam Smith is Harry Styles: The Making of a Modern Man and it follows the normal style of a historical biography. It details the development of a thoroughly modern man with incredible charisma.

A25. Harry co-hosted the glitzy Met Gala appearance event in 2019, alongside Lady Gaga. He embraced the event's theme of "In America: A Lexicon of Fashion" with his striking and gender-fluid ensemble.

A26. Harry's second album was titled "Fine Line". The album received critical acclaim and commercial success, further establishing his artistic identity.

A27. Harry has a tattoo of a large butterfly on his stomach.

A28. Harry's first tattoo was on his inner left arm, or bicep, which he had done on his eighteenth birthday. It started out as just an outline of star, but he eventually had it filled in with black ink.

A29. Harry has a tattoo of a pair of swallows on his upper chest.

A30. Harry once lost a lot of money playing roulette, specifically on Black 17, so he got a permanent reminder of it.

Here is the next set of questions.

31. Where was the music video to "Golden" mainly filmed?
    A. France
    B. Germany
    C. Italy
    D. Spain

32. Which magazine named Harry "2020's Best Dressed Man"?
    A. GQ
    B. Esquire
    C. Loaded
    D. Red

33. Which song includes the lyrics "I'm out of my head, and I know that you're scared because hearts get broken"?
    A. Adore You
    B. Falling
    C. Golden
    D. Watermelon Sugar

34. What is the title of the documentary film on Harry that was released in 2021?
    A. Harry Styles – Behind The Album
    B. Harry Styles – Behind The Covers

C. Harry Styles – Behind The Scenes

D. Harry Styles – Behind The Sofa

35. What is the title of the movie that features "Sweet Creature" on its soundtrack?

A. Fifty Shades Of Grey

B. Fifty Shades Darker

C. Fifty Shades Freed

D. Fifty Shades Trilogy

36. What is Harry's favourite perfume?

A. Chanel Coco Mademoiselle

B. Jean Paul Gaultier Classique

C. Jimmy Choo Flash

D. Tom Ford Black Orchid

37. What is Harry's favourite type of music?

A. Hip Hop

B. Pop

C. Rock and Roll

D. Rhythm and Blues

38. What is Harry's favourite sport?

A. Cricket

B. Football

C. Golf

D. Tennis

39.Which chat show did Harry host and perform on in 2019?
    A. Jimmy Kimmel Live
    B. Saturday Night Live
    C. The Late Show with Stephen Colbert
    D. The Tonight Show with Jimmy Fallon

40.Which charity did Harry donate a part of his earnings from his debut solo tour to?
    A. Greenpeace
    B. Help Refugees
    C. Unicef
    D. WWF

Here is the latest set of answers.

A31. The music video for "Golden" was filmed on the stunning Amalfi Coast in Italy. The picturesque locations and Harry's charismatic presence make it a visually captivating video.

A32. Harry was named "2020's Best Dressed Man" by British GQ, recognising his fearless and boundary-pushing fashion choices.

A33. The song "Golden" contains the lyrics "I'm out of my head, and I know that you're scared because hearts get broken."

A34. The documentary film "Harry Styles: Behind the Album" provides an intimate look into the making of his album "Fine Line," featuring revealing behind-the-scenes footage.

A35. Fifty Shades Darker featured "Sweet Creature" on its soundtrack. Fifty Shades Darker is part of the Fifty Shades series which includes Fifty Shades of Grey.

A36. Harry's favourite perfume is Tom Ford Black Orchid. He has said that he loves the smell of it.

A37. Harry's favourite type of music is pop. He has said that he loves the catchy melodies and the upbeat songs.

A38. Harry's favourite sport is football. He has said that he loves the excitement of the game and the camaraderie of the team.

A39. Harry made a fabulous guest appearance on The Tonight Show Starring Jimmy Fallon in 2021, and at one stage acted as the host of the show.

A40. Harry donated a substantial portion of his earnings from his debut solo tour to Help Refugees, an organization that supports those affected by the refugee crisis.

Hope you're having fun. Here is the next set of questions.

41. Which iconic band does Harry often sing cover songs of at his live performances?
    A. Fleetwood Mac
    B. Led Zeppelin
    C. Queen
    D. The Rolling Stones

42. What is the name of Harry's third album?
    A. Harry's Garden
    B. Harry's Gone
    C. Harry's Home
    D. Harry's House

43. What music video features Harry befriending a fish?
    A. Adore You
    B. Golden
    C. To Be So Lonely
    D. Treat People With Kindness

44. What song features the line "I got a good feeling, I'm just takin' it all in"?
    A. Falling

B. She
C. To Be So Lonely
D. Treat People With Kindness

45. What song includes the line "Do you know who you are?" regularly?
    A. Cherry
    B. Falling
    C. Fine Line
    D. Golden

46. Who did Harry support in 2020 by designing and selling a limited-edition T shirt?
    A. World Bank Group
    B. World Food Programme
    C. World Health Organization
    D. World Wildlife Fund

47. Where was the music video for "Lights Up" filmed?
    A. Mexico City
    B. New York City
    C. Panama City
    D. Sun City

48. How many awards did Harry win at the 2023 Brit Awards?

A. 1
B. 2
C. 3
D. 4

49. What was the name of Harry's first pet?
    A. A cat called Whiskers
    B. A dog named Blue
    C. A fish named Wanda
    D. A hamster named Hammy

50. What is Harry's favourite food?
    A. Salami
    B. Sausages
    C. Steak
    D. Sushi

Here is the latest set of answers.

A41. Harry pays homage to the legendary rock band Fleetwood Mac by covering their songs "The Chain" and "Landslide" during his live performances, showcasing his vocal range and paying tribute to a legendary band. Mick Fleetwood and band member Stevie Nicks said Harry's version of 'The Chain' is the best cover they've ever heard.

A42. Harry's third album is called Harry's House. It was released in May 2022 and went on to top the charts very quickly in multiple countries.

A43. The music video for "Adore You" showcases Harry's storytelling abilities and whimsical nature as he befriends a fish and embarks on a journey to make it happy.

A44. The song "Treat People With Kindness" includes the line "I got a good feeling, I'm just takin' it all in, Floating up and dreamin', droppin' into the deep end."

A45. The song "Fine Line" includes the thought-provoking line "Do you know who you are?" as a central theme.

A46. Harry supported the World Health Organization COVID-19 Solidarity Response Fund by designing and selling merchandise with the slogan "Stay Home. Stay Safe. Protect Each Other," raising funds for global efforts to combat the pandemic.

A47. The majority of the music video for "Lights Up" was filmed in Mexico City. The video shows Styles dancing shirtless in a crowd of sweat-drenched people with them often draping themselves over Harry.

A48. Harry swept the board and won a total of four awards at the 2023 Brit Awards. He won all four of his categories , winning best song – for As It Was, best album (Harry's House), best pop/R&B act and the best artist award.

A49. Harry's first pet was a dog named Blue, who he got when he was just 10 years old.

A50. Harry's favourite food is sushi. He has said that he loves the taste of the fish and the rice.

Let's have some movie related questions.

51. What was the name of the film in which Harry made his acting debut?
    A. Dark Knight Rises
    B. Dunkirk
    C. Inception
    D. Interstellar

52. What was the name of the character Harry played?
    A. Alan
    B. Albert
    C. Alex
    D. Alfred

53. Who was the director of the film in which Harry made his acting debut?
    A. Christopher Nolan
    B. Martin Scorsese
    C. Steven Spielberg
    D. Quentin Tarantino

54. Which movie marked Harry's second collaboration with director Christopher Nolan?
    A. Justice League
    B. Oppenheimer

C. Tenet

D. The Dark Knight Rises

55. Who was the director in the movie Don't Worry Darling which starred Harry?

   A. Gemma Chan

   B. KiKi Layne

   C. Florence Pugh

   D. Olivia Wilde

56. What was the name of the character Harry played in the movie Don't Worry Darling?

   A. Jack

   B. Jake

   C. Jim

   D. Joe

57. What is the name of the 2022 romantic drama film based on the novel by Bethan Roberts which Harry starred in?

   A. My Painter

   B. My Parole Officer

   C. My Pathologist

   D. My Policeman

58. Who is Harry's favourite actor?

   A. Leonardo Di Caprio

   B. Tom Hanks

C. Brad Pitt
D. Ryan Reynolds

59. Who is Harry's favourite actress?
    A. Cate Blanchett
    B. Jennifer Lawrence
    C. Julianne Moore
    D. Emma Stone

60. What is Harry's favourite movie?
    A. Goodfellas
    B. Pulp Fiction
    C. The Lord Of The Rings
    D. The Shawshank Redemption

Here are the answers to the movie related questions.

A51. Harry made his acting debut in the 2017 war film "Dunkirk". It was nominated for a Best Picture Oscar.

A52. Harry played the part of Alex Stone, a British soldier stranded on the beaches of Dunkirk during the Second World War.

A53. Christopher Nolan directed the movie Dunkirk.

A54. Harry worked with director Christopher Nolan for the second time in the 2020 science fiction action thriller movie called "Tenet".

A55. Olivia Wilde is credited with being director of the movie "Don't Worry Darling".

A56. Harry played the part of Jack in the movie "Don't Worry Darling".

A57. Harry had a leading role in My Policeman, a film based on the novel of the same name by Bethan Roberts. The film had its world premiere at the Toronto International Film Festival in September 2022, and Harry received good reviews for his acting. He said,

"It was such a beautiful script. The complexity of Tom made him a really interesting character to play."

A58. Harry's favourite actor is Leonardo DiCaprio. He has said that he loves DiCaprio's acting range and his commitment to his roles.

A59. Harry's favourite actress is Cate Blanchett. He has said that he loves Blanchett's beauty and her talent.

A60. Harry's favourite movie is The Shawshank Redemption. He has said that he loves the story and the characters.

Let's have some questions about Harry's favourite things.

61. What is Harry's favourite colour nail polish?
    A. Black
    B. Blue
    C. Pink
    D. Red

62. What is Harry's favourite flower?
    A. Lily
    B. Peony
    C. Rose
    D. Sunflower

63. What is Harry's favourite place to travel to?
    A. Berlin
    B. Madrid
    C. Paris
    D. Rome

64. What is Harry's favourite song by another artist?
    A. Hallelujah by Leonard Cohen
    B. I Will Survive by Gloria Gaynor

C. Imagine by John Lennon
D. It's Raining Men by Cyndi Lauper

65. What is Harry's favourite pastime?
    A. Golfing
    B. Playing video games
    C. Running
    D. Swimming

66. What is Harry's favourite thing to do on tour?
    A. Go Swimming
    B. Meet The Fans
    C. Party After The Show
    D. See The Sights

67. What is Harry's favourite thing to do on a hot day?
    A. Go To The Beach
    B. Eat Ice Cream
    C. Have A Picnic
    D. Swim

68. What is Harry's favourite thing to do on a cold day?
    A. Build A Snowman
    B. Go For A Run
    C. Go Skiing

D. Stay Indoors

69. What is Harry's favourite thing to do when he's not working?
    A. Design Clothes
    B. Hang Out With Friends
    C. Read Books
    D. Write Music

70. What is Harry's favourite book?
    A. The Great Gatsby
    B. The Jungle Book
    C. The Lord Of The Rings
    D. To Kill A Mockingbird

Here is the latest set of answers. Answers to some of Harry's favourite things.

A61. Harry has been seen wearing blue nail polish on multiple occasions. He has said that he loves the way it looks and that it makes him feel confident.

A62. Harry has said that he loves sunflowers because they are "so happy and cheerful."

A63. Harry's favourite city to travel to is Paris. He has said that he loves the city's beauty and its rich history

A64. Harry's favourite song by another artist is "Hallelujah" by Leonard Cohen. He has said that he loves the lyrics and the melody.

A65. Harry's favourite thing to do in his free time is play video games. He has said that he loves the challenge and the competition

A66. Harry's favourite thing to do on tour is meet the fans. He has said that he loves hearing their stories and making them happy.

A67. Harry' favourite thing to do on a hot day is go to the beach. He has said that he loves the feeling of the sand between his toes and the sound of the waves crashing.

A68. Harry's favourite thing to do on a cold day is stay inside and cuddle up with a blanket. He has said that he loves the feeling of being warm and cozy.

A69. Harry's favourite thing to do when he's not working is spend time with his family and friends. He has said that they are the most important people in his life.

A70. Harry's favourite book is The Great Gatsby. He has said that he loves the writing style and the characters.

Here is the next set of questions.

71. What song includes the line "Don't you call him what you used to call me"?
    A. Cherry
    B. Falling
    C. Fine Line
    D. Golden

72. What song includes the line "I'd walk through fire for you"?
    A. Adore You
    B. Falling
    C. Golden
    D. Watermelon Sugar

73. Which album contains the songs "Adore You" and "Falling"?
    A. Behind The Album
    B. Fine Line
    C. Harry's House
    D. Harry Styles

74. Which of these is a real song of Harry's?
    A. Music for a Chinese restaurant
    B. Music for an Indian restaurant
    C. Music for an Italian restaurant

D. Music for a Sushi restaurant

75. What is Harry's favourite colour?
    A. Blue
    B. Green
    C. Red
    D. Yellow

76. Which of these girls' names is a real song of Harry's?
    A. Madeline
    B. Mary
    C. Martha
    D. Matilda

77. What did Harry treat himself to when "Up All Night" reached Number 1 in America?
    A. A mattress
    B. A pair of Jimmy Choo shoes
    C. A pair of Ray Ban sunglasses
    D. A pearl necklace

78. What foreign language can Harry speak?
    A. French
    B. German
    C. Italian
    D. Spanish

79. Who did Harry duet with at the 2022 Coachella music festival?
    A. Celine Dion
    B. Faith Hill
    C. Dolly Parton
    D. Shani Twain

80. What does Harry enjoy cooking the most?
    A. Sausages
    B. Spaghetti
    C. Steak
    D. Swordfish

Here is the latest set of answers.

A71. "Cherry" features the line "Don't you call him what you used to call me" expressing self-awareness and reflection on personal flaws within a relationship.

A72. "Adore You" features the line "I'd walk through fire for you, just let me adore you" expressing deep affection and devotion towards someone.

A73. The album "Fine Line" features the hit songs "Adore You" and "Falling".

A74. "Music for a Sushi Restaurant" is a song from Harry's album Harry's House.

A75. Harry's favourite colour is blue. He has said that he loves the colour because it reminds him of the ocean.

A76. "Matilda" is a song from Harry's album Harry's House.

A77. Harry treated himself to a mattress after Up All Night reached the top of the charts in America.

A78. Harry can speak conversational French.

A79. Harry performed two duets with Shania Twain at the 2022 Coachella music festival "Man, I feel like a woman" and "You're still the one". A year later Harry was back at Coachella headlining the festival in front of over 100,000 people.

A80. Harry's favourite food to cook is spaghetti. He has said that he loves the simplicity of the dish and the fact that it is always a crowd-pleaser.

Let's have some opening line questions.

81. Which song starts with the following line "Put a price on emotion, I'm looking for something to buy"?
    A. Adore You
    B. Fine Line
    C. Golden
    D. Sign Of The Times

82. Which song starts with the following line "Tastes like strawberries on a summer evenin'"?
    A. Cherry
    B. Late Night Talking
    C. Sweet Creature
    D. Watermelon Sugar

83. Which song starts with the following line "Don't blame me for falling, I was just a little boy"?
    A. Falling
    B. Love Of My Life
    C. Satellite
    D. To Be So Lonely

84. Which song starts with the following line "Open up your eyes, shut your mouth and see"?
  A. Canyon Moon
  B. Music For A Sushi Restaurant
  C. Only Angel
  D. Woman

85. Which song starts with the following line "I'm in my bed. And you're not here"?
  A. Cherry
  B. Falling
  C. Late Night Talking
  D. Treat People With Kindness

86. Which song starts with the following line "Gotta see it to believe it, sky never looked so blue"?
  A. Canyon Moon
  B. Lights Up
  C. Satellite
  D. Sign Of The Times

87. Which song starts with the following line "Same lips red, same eyes blue, same white shirt, couple more tattoos"?
  A. Carolina
  B. Cherry

    C. Sweet Creature

    D. Two Ghosts

88. Which song starts with the following line "Holdin' me back, gravity's holdin' me back"?

    A. Adore You

    B. As It Was

    C. Golden

    D. Satellite

89. Which song starts with the following line "I'm selfish, I know, but I don't ever want to see you with him"?

    A. Golden

    B. Kiwi

    C. She

    D. Woman

90. Which song starts with the following line "What do you mean? I'm sorry by the way. Never coming back down"?

    A. Adore You

    B. Late Night Talking

    C. Lights Up

    D. Treat People With Kindness

Here are the answers to the opening lyrics section.

A81. Fine Line starts with the line "Put a price on emotion, I'm looking for something to buy."

A82. Watermelon Sugar starts with thew line "Tastes like strawberries on a summer evenin.'"

A83. To Be So Lonely starts with the line "Don't blame me for falling, I was just a little boy."

A84. Only Angel starts with the line "Open up your eyes, shut your mouth and see."

A85. Falling starts with the line "I'm in my bed. And you're not here."

A86. Canyon Moon starts with the line "Gotta see it to believe it, sky never looked so blue."

A87. Two Ghosts starts with the line "Same lips red, same eyes blue, same white shirt, couple more tattoos."

A88. As It Was starts with the line "Holdin' me back, gravity's holdin' me back."

A89. Woman starts with the line "I'm selfish, I know, but I don't ever want to see you with him."

A90. Lights Up starts with the line "What do you mean? I'm sorry by the way. Never coming back down."

OK, here goes with the last set of questions.

91. Which of these musical instruments can Harry play?
    A. Didgeridoo
    B. Harp
    C. Hurdy Gurdy
    D. Kazoo

92. What is the name of Harry's make up collection?
    A. Pleasant
    B. Pleasing
    C. Pleasers
    D. Pleasure

93. How tall is Harry?
    A. 5 feet 6 inches
    B. 5 feet 9 inches
    C. 6 feet
    D. 6 feet 3 inches

94. Who has a matching tattoo with Harry?
    A. Lewis Capaldi
    B. Shawn Mendes
    C. Ed Sheeran
    D. Sam Smith

95. How many Grammy awards has Harry won?
    A. 1
    B. 2
    C. 3
    D. 4

96. Who was the director for the music video to "Golden"?
    A. Dan Emmerson
    B. Colin Read
    C. Henry Scholfield
    D. Ben Winston

97. What song did Harry sing in his initial audition for X Factor?
    A. Isn't She Lovely
    B. Lovely Day
    C. Sweet And Lovely
    D. Where Do You Go To My Lovely

98. What was One Direction's debut album?
    A. Four
    B. Midnight Memories
    C. Take Me Home
    D. Up All Night

99. Which Ariana Grande song did Harry co-write?
   A. Dangerous Woman
   B. Just A Little Bit Of Your Heart
   C. Love Me Harder
   D. My Everything

100. Which music video featured Harry flying?
   A. Adore You
   B. Falling
   C. Only Angel
   D. Sign Of The Times

101. What does Harry call his fans?
   A. Barmy Army
   B. Fanatics
   C. Harries
   D. Stylers

Here is the final set of answers.

A91. Harry can play the kazoo, apparently quite well by all accounts. A kazoo is a simple musical instrument, made up of a hollow pipe with a hole in it.

A92. Harry's make-up brand is called Pleasing. The marketing blurb states "Pleasing's mission is to bring joyful experiences and products to all, finding inspiration in nature as well as the multitude of unique identities in the founder's life."

A93. Harry is 6 feet tall. In metric this is 1.83 metres.

A94. Harry and Ed Sheeran both loved the TV show Pingu, and when Ed went to get a tattoo of Pingu done, he brought his friend Harry along, which resulted in the pair getting matching Pingu ink. Ed has a cartoon penguin, and Harry has the word Pingu.

A95. Harry has won a total of three Grammy Awards. In 2023 he won Best Pop Vocal Album for Harry's House, Album of the Year for

Harry's House; and in 2021 he won Pop Solo Performance for 'Watermelon Sugar'.

A96. Ben Winston directed the music video for the song "Golden." He had previously directed several of One Direction's music videos.

A97. When the show originally aired, way back in 2010, Harry's audition featured an a cappella rendition of the Stevie Wonder classic, "Isn't She Lovely."

A98. One Direction's debut album was entitled "Up All Night". It was a huge success, topping the charts in sixteen countries. It became the third best-selling album of 2012 with sales of over four million copies worldwide.

A99. Harry co-wrote Just a Little Bit of Your Heart with Johan Carlsson for Ariana Grande.

A100. In the stunning music video for "Sign Of The Times", filmed in Scotland, Harry is seen flying through the air dressed in his classic Chelsea boots and skinny jeans combo.

A101. Harry calls his millions of fans "Harries" although journalists often refer to us as "Stylers". Give yourself a point for either answer.

That's a great question to finish with.

That's it. I hope you enjoyed this book, and I hope you got most of the answers right. I also hope you learnt some new things about Hazza!

If you have any comments or if you saw anything wrong, please email harry@glowwormpress.com and we'll get the book updated.

If this book was a gift, there is just one thing left to do and that's to ask the person who got this book for you to leave a positive review on Amazon saying what you think of Harry.

We are told he loves reading his reviews.

Many thanks in advance.

Printed in Great Britain
by Amazon

33822746R00036